Praise for *Love, Tiara, And A Cupcake*

A pastor and comedian who quotes the Bible, along with stories of Elvis, pimento cheese, and Kmart, Susan Sparks is like a hilarious friend who teaches you valuable life lessons while you're too busy smiling to notice. With humor and grace, Susan unlocks the key to finding happiness in the little things, and tells you why love, a tiara, and a cupcake are all you need to spark joy in your life.

—**Tracy Beckerman**, Syndicated Columnist and Author, "Lost in Suburbia: A Momoir"

Love, A Tiara, And A Cupcake:

Three Secrets to Finding Happy

REV. SUSAN SPARKS

FREE GIFTS

I'm so honored that you decided to buy my book!
To say thank you, I have three free gifts for you:

1) A few of my favorite cupcake recipes (see appendix in the back)

2) A make-your-own-tiara kit (thank you, FirstPalette.com!)
https://www.firstpalette.com/printable/princess-crown.html

3) A special "Love, a Tiara, and a Cupcake Journal" where you can think through and write your answers to the questions at the end of each chapter.

To access your free journal
https://mailchi.mp/susansparks.com/love-a-tiara-and-a-cupcake

Or go to:

https://mailchi.mp/susansparks.com/love-a-tiara-and-a-cupcake

Or scan this QR code with your phone:

ENJOY!

ALSO BY SUSAN SPARKS

Laugh Your Way to Grace:
Reclaiming the Spiritual Power of Humor

Preaching Punchlines: The Ten Commandments of Comedy

Miracle on 31st Street:
Christmas Cheer Every Day of the Year—
Grinch to Gratitude in 26 Days!

Grace-Filled Gratitude: A 40-Day Joy Journal
with Inspirational Scriptures

TABLE OF CONTENTS

DEDICATION

*This book is dedicated to one of my favorite cupcakes:
my delicious wee grandson Jamie,
who simply radiates joy and love.*

ACKNOWLEDGMENTS

I have so many to thank for the creation of this book. First, I must thank Sylvia Meincke and the Women's Christian Book Club in Daytona Beach, Florida. Inspired by one of my 2020 nationally syndicated columns entitled, "All You Need is Love, a Tiara, and a Cupcake," they decided to gather for a book club picnic wearing tiaras, eating cupcakes, and using my column as their discussion piece. They sent me a photograph of the picnic, and when I saw it, I knew it—that would be my next book! Several months later, voila! *Love, a Tiara, and a Cupcake: Three Secrets to Finding Happy* was born.

Many thanks to those who helped create and launch this book, including my launch team, my editor Brooks Becker, my cover designer Christos Angelidakis, and my formatter Rachael Cox.

Heartfelt thanks to my beautiful community of faith, Madison Avenue Baptist Church in New York City, for sitting through twenty years of my sermons. A number of these chapters were pulled from those sermons, and it has been my greatest honor to preach every Sunday from that historic pulpit.

Most of all, I'd like to thank my family and friends, who are always full of support and encouragement, and my husband (and most beloved cupcake), Toby Solberg, who never fails to make me smile and bring me joy.

INTRODUCTION

How do you hold on to hope in the midst of despair?

To answer that question, you can read every one of the seven trillion self-help books on Amazon. Or you can spend hours listening to YouTube videos and Ted Talks. Or you can lie on the couch in microwave booties, binge-watching all six seasons of *Downton Abbey* (plus the film).

My preference, however, is to go the simple route.

All you need is love, a tiara, and a cupcake.

It's a three-part secret I discovered while negotiating my own moments of despair and difficulty. From losing my parents to going through a divorce to surviving breast cancer, I've learned that in any place of pain, you need to remember three things: Your purpose, your worth, and your smile. And the perfect metaphors for these three secret weapons are love, a tiara, and a cupcake. I've divided the book into three separate sections dedicated to each.

Notwithstanding the order of the title, let's start with the cupcake. I mean come on . . . who doesn't love a cupcake? Maybe it reminds us of childhood. Maybe it's because we love sweets. Or maybe it's because they're tiny. Whatever the reason, a cupcake just makes you happy. In fact, food editor Anne Byrn said, "When you look at a cupcake, you have to smile!"

We all have our favorite cupcake recipes that include ingredients that fill us with happiness and joy. My favorite is a tie between my friend Turner's Blackberry Buttercream Cupcakes and, for the more adventurous, "Knock-You-Naked Margarita Cupcakes" (the perfect choice for an ordained minister). The recipes for both, as well as other fabulous cupcake favorites, are included in the appendix of the book.

In addition to the literal cake treats, we also have our cupcakes of life—that person, place, or thing that fills us with happiness and joy. What's your cupcake?

Whatever it is, you must hold on to it for all you're worth. To be sure, the world will do everything in its power to take your joy, wear you down, and steal your cupcake.

One of my favorite books is *The Boy, the Mole, the Fox, and the Horse* by Charles Macksey, and in it is one of my favorite quotes: "Sometimes just getting up and carrying on is brave and magnificent."

Amen to that!

Just so you know, I wrote this book in the middle of the COVID-19 crisis. However, the lessons are universal and apply to any time of difficulty in life. Bottom line? It takes a load of courage to live fully. That's why in the "Cupcake" section I include chapters on things like anger, loss, negativity, fear, and worry (to which I've dedicated three full chapters). These are all things that can steal your joy. Of course, we also talk about boundaries, patience, and the power of a smile—all things that can regenerate your joy!

In addition to claiming our cupcake, we also need a reminder that we matter: a tiara. Everybody knows that you need a little swagger to wear a tiara. You need a little pride in yourself to wear a crown. These days, however, self-respect is hard won in the fight against shame.

People love to shame. But we also know, at least intellectually, that the need to dishonor another comes from that person's own shame. It's driven by their own fears, their own self-loathing, and their resentment about what's not right in their life. As the old saying goes, "Mediocrity attacks excellence."

Here's the good news: we all have the power to refuse to be shamed. Personally, I use the Psalmists to reinforce that power. Those ancient writers wore some seriously big tiaras. Think about Psalm 34:5: "Those who look to the Lord are radiant, and their faces shall never be ashamed."

To help us to claim our worth, I include chapters in the "Tiara" section about overcoming mistakes, faith, letting go, and setting priorities. My goal is to get us to remember who and whose we are. You are a child of God. When you were born, God crowned you with a radiant tiara—a holy stamp of approval, a sign of your belonging. Wear. It. Proudly.

So we find our cupcake, don our holy tiara, and then take the most important step by using those powers to march into the midst of the world's excruciating pain and begin to love. The power of human love is dazzling. As the chapters in the "Love" section teach, love can build bridges, highlight our potential, give us perspective, and usher in miracles. Never has the world—the human heart— needed it more.

That said, the human heart is an amazing thing. Science has estimated that within an average human lifespan, it beats approximately two billion times.

Here's my question: How do you want to spend them?

Do you want your heart burning through those beats in fear, stress, and anger?

Or do you want every one of those precious rhythms to be a beat of love and joy?

It's a painful, aching time in this life. But even now, we can be brave and magnificent. Out of the chaos of these times can come a better day. And it's up to us—you and me—to usher that day in.

Find a comfy place to curl up with the book, taking time at the end of each chapter to answer the questions in your free journal (see links in "Free Gifts" section above). Better yet, get some friends together and use the book as an excuse for a party! Bring cupcakes, wear your tiaras, and share what you've read and learned.

Solo or with friends, join me! Find your joy, don your radiance, and open your arms in compassion. Remember, three simple things can bring us happiness and truly change the world: Love, a tiara, and a cupcake.

A CUPCAKE

The Weaponization of Pimento Cheese

"The person who has the most influence over your life is the person you refuse to forgive."

- Anonymous

There have been many times when the world tried to steal my joy. The worst example?

The time the TSA stole my pimento cheese.

They could have taken my laptop, my wallet, or even my *People* magazine with photos from the royal wedding. I wouldn't have cared. But my pimento cheese? It was an unspeakable loss.

I was heading home to New York City from a lovely visit with family in North Carolina. As always, I was bringing back a Southern treat to remind me of my roots and make me less lonely when I landed. On this trip, I packed a small container of my all-time favorite food: Palmetto pimento cheese.

Now, for those of you who are thinking, "It's a sandwich spread, Susan, get over it," let me clarify. You can't buy this stuff in NYC. Oh sure, New Yorkers *claim* they have it. But the stuff they sell is, well, fake. It's an odd, tasteless, Yankee version that I refuse to consume. The bottom line is that for me, a Southerner living in NYC, authentic pimento cheese is a priceless commodity.

Back to the theft. I entered the Raleigh TSA PreCheck, placed my bag on the conveyor belt, and walked through the metal detector. When I got on the other side, I noticed the X-ray attendant squinting at the screen, her lips pursed.

"I need a bag search!" she yelled, plopping my sack into a separate bin.

My mind raced through the litany of possibly "dangerous" things in my bag:

Tweezers? No.

Loofah? It's scratchy, so maybe . . .

Hairbrush? It has firm bristles, so you could probably bruise someone's scalp with it.

Just as I was about to cough up the brush, I watched in horror as the TSA agent lifted out the plastic bag with my container of pimento cheese.

"You can't take this on the plane," he said, heading to the trash.

"It's pimento cheese!" I wailed. "And really good pimento cheese! Palmetto! You can't buy that up north!"

"It's a liquid and not allowed," he snapped.

I watched as my beloved was summarily tossed in the trash. Wonderful deliciousness wasted—struck down in its prime. And for what? Protection of the free world? An effort to curb the weaponization of pimento cheese?

I walked over to the trashcan and peered in, like a mourner looking into a grave. All of a sudden, I flashed to the scripture from my last sermon: "For our present troubles are small and won't last very long . . . We fix our gaze on things that cannot be seen. For the things we see now will soon be gone, but the things we cannot see will last forever" (2 Corinthians 4:17-18). Momentarily comforted, I said a short prayer over the pimento cheese, then turned and walked away.

On the flight back, I couldn't stop thinking about the loss of my beloved. It was so unfair—so unjust. I pulled a newspaper out of my bag to get my mind off the tragedy, and the headlines quickly put my suffering in perspective. People all over the world were facing unfair, unjust losses. Some had lost their savings, health, or job. Others had a dire loss of food or clean water. Still others had experienced loss of life, many through bombs and bullets.

I put the paper down and stared out the window at the tiny dot of Philadelphia passing below. Maybe I needed to lighten up on the TSA. This certainly wasn't a life-threatening loss. In fact, their actions, crazy as they were, were meant to prevent loss. They were just doing their job as best they could.

I was within a hair's breadth of forgiveness when the horrible reality came rushing back: I was doomed to eat tasteless Yankee pimento cheese until my next visit home. I nestled back in my Delta aisle seat, stewing on my anger until a new, more sinister question popped into my mind:

What were those TSA agents in Raleigh having for lunch?

Questions to Consider:

- What loss have you experienced recently?
- Was there a reason for it? A greater good?
- If not, can you forgive what or who you believe to be the "cause" of this loss? Can you transform this loss into something joyful?

Check Your Weapons at the Door

"Anger after 30 seconds is ego."

- My recent fortune cookie

Out in Wyoming, I had an unfortunate motorcycle collision ... with a bug. You might think something like, "Aww, how sad for the bug." In fact, I was the one that ended up visiting a local hospital. Although the bug incident was jarring, the large sign at the entrance of the clinic—"Check Your Weapons at the Door"—was more alarming. Who knew that when seeing a doctor, one needed to come packing heat?

The bug injury healed, but I've never forgotten that sign. Over time, I have decided that the message "check your weapons at the door" is great advice for life.

There are a lot of weapons floating around these days. On the international scene, there are nukes, drone strikes, and WMDs (weapons of mass destruction). In the United States, there's the scourge of automatic weapons. But there's also an equally scary and perhaps even more dangerous weapon at large in the world: the human tongue. And anger can steal your joy faster than almost anything else.

We've all been on the receiving and the giving end of words that sting like hitting a bug at seventy miles per hour—words of anger, fear, or hate that can tear relationships, families, and hearts apart. Proverbs 12:18 explains it like this: "The words of the reckless pierce like swords, but the tongue of the wise brings healing."

Every one of us is packing heat. The question is whether we will check that weapon at the door.

The unfortunate truth is that human beings love to run their mouths, to tell others what they think, to lecture others about what is right and wrong. Just look at all the talking heads on television. But we're just as guilty.

We fling words the same way I cook spaghetti: sloppily. Never an exacting kind of cook, I throw the noodles against the wall and see what sticks. As you can imagine, I have a pretty messy kitchen.

Like with spaghetti, we randomly throw out words and see what sticks. But unlike spaghetti, words always stick, and we can't take them back. And please understand those words can be both spoken and written. Think about texting, emailing, and posting on social media, especially the vicious words exchanged on sites like Facebook.

I think the Psalmists were right: "Set a guard over my mouth, Lord; keep watch over the door of my lips" (Psalm 141:3). If only we would check our harsh and angry words at the doors of our mouths before we spoke them. God forbid we actually listen before we speak.

The author Steven Covey wrote, "Most people do not listen with the intent to understand, they listen with the intent to reply." It's true. We want to have something sparkly and intelligent to say in return. But more so, we want to be right.

In any conversation, there are two parts: the mouth and the heart. When we listen to reply, we're listening only to what comes out of the mouth. When we truly listen to understand, we hear not only from the mouth, but also the heart.

Power does not come from weapons targeted at intimidation and destruction, such as WMD's or words. Power comes from deep, empathetic listening with an intent to truly understand.

I can't help but think about an experience my husband and I had at a hospital right before he had back surgery. We were in a room with another patient who was awaiting rotator cuff surgery, a curtain separating us. The doctor for the other patient came in and in a clipped, brusque voice said, "Yours is the most painful surgery I do. You are not going to like me very much after this. Any questions before we go in?" (Direct quote—I swear.) There was a stunned silence from behind the curtain after he walked out.

Within a few seconds, our doctor breezed in with a huge smile. "Hi! I am really excited to do this surgery. You're going to feel so much better after this. Come on—let's go! We're going to make you taller." We both laughed hysterically, then Toby was rolled out past the other patient, who was close to tears. It was a lesson in the destructive and healing potential of our words.

In the end, I am sorry for that Wyoming bug. But he did not die in vain. He (and the sign at the hospital) made me think. Slinging negative words, flinging angry sentiments, and constantly fighting to be right will get us nowhere. We have to stop this arms race. Let's check our weapons at the door and give each other—and this old world—a momentary chance to heal.

Questions to Consider:

- Have you flung out angry words recently? Do you regret it?
- Have you felt the sting of angry words from someone recently?
- What are three ways you can check your weapons/words at the door?

Jesus and Dr. Seuss:
A Conversation on Worry

"Worry is interest paid on trouble before it is due."

- **William R. Inge**, *English author, priest, and professor*

We're going to talk about worry for the next three chapters. Why? Because it's become one of our national pastimes. Baseball, football, and worrying.

To get us started, let's use two of my favorite people: Jesus and Dr. Seuss. Jesus because . . . well, he's Jesus. And Dr. Seuss because he is an unsung hero of wisdom.

We tend to dismiss Dr. Seuss as a simple children's writer who made funny rhymes. In reality, he was a Dartmouth and Oxford–educated writer who won two Academy Awards, two Emmy Awards, a Peabody, and a Pulitzer Prize. Not bad.

So, today, let's put Jesus and Dr. Seuss in conversation for three lessons on worry.

Lesson #1: Focus on today.

In Matthew 6:34, Jesus says, "Do not worry about tomorrow. For tomorrow will bring worries of its own. Today's trouble is enough for today." Well, amen to that. Life is hard—particularly now. That said, sometimes we make it worse on ourselves by making up extra stuff to worry about, like what might happen tomorrow or what could happen the day after tomorrow.

However, Jesus taught us that we can control what we think by focusing on today. Here's an idea: try putting your worries in a box. Literally. Keep a running list of everything you are worried about, then slip the list inside a small box and designate fifteen minutes a day when you can take out the papers and wallow in your worry list. Then, at the end of that time, return the worries to the box and return to your life.

Does it stop the anxiety? No, but it cuts it down to size.

Dr. Seuss explained it like this: "I've heard there are troubles of more than one kind; some come from ahead, and some come from behind. But I've brought a big bat. I'm all ready, you see; now my troubles are going to have troubles with me!"

Lesson #2: Worry is a waste of time.

In Matthew 6:27, Jesus says, "Can any of you by worrying add a single hour to your span of life?"

Can we? No.

So why are we worrying? We can't worry a project at work into success. Worry scatters our attention, zaps our strength, and prevents us from operating at our best. We can't worry a mistake away. We can only learn from it and move on. We can't worry a pandemic away. In fact, worry can make it worse, as studies show that worry can compromise our immune system.

It's not surprising that the word worry comes from an Anglo-Saxon word meaning to strangle or to choke. We all know what that feels like—that sensation of tightness that comes over us when we are worrying in the middle of the night.

The irony is that if we stop worrying, we might be able to take some steps forward on the things we are worried about! Dr. Seuss adds, "And when things start to happen, don't worry. Don't stew. Just go right along. You'll start happening too."

Lesson #3: Worry or believe—you can't do both.

It's easy in times like these to worry, or, worse yet, get angry at God and ask why this is happening to you. News flash: Life is not a holy contract in which God promises a calm passage. What God does promise is a safe landing: "When you pass through the rivers, they will not sweep over you. When you walk through the fire, you will not be burned" (Isaiah 43:2).

Therefore, instead of asking God why this is happening TO you, thank God for being WITH you. No matter where we find ourselves in life, it's still life—it's still a gift. And we must honor that gift in all we do. Dr. Seuss explained it this way: "Sometimes you'll never know the value of a moment until it becomes a memory."

Will these lessons make our worries disappear? No. But they can certainly help us manage them better. Remember, "I can do everything through him who gives me strength" (Philippians 4:13). Or, as Dr. Seuss promised, "And will you succeed? Yes! You will, indeed! (98 and ¾ percent guaranteed.)"

Questions to Consider:

- What are you worried about today?

- What do you get from worrying about it? Is it worth your health? Your joy?

- Worry or believe. Which do you choose?

Dancing Skeletons

"Named must your fear be before banish it you can."

- Yoda

"It's just a coat hanger, Susan," my mother would sigh, pointing at the flimsy wire triangle.

But I knew better.

It was not JUST a coat hanger. Together with the other hangers, it formed the lair of the evil skeleton who lurked in my closet.

By day, his cave looked all too innocent, Garanimals and Sesame Street fashions hanging peacefully side by side. But by night, the clothes mysteriously faded away and the wiry hangers morphed into the bony fingers of my enemy. Every cell in my body urged me to jump up, slam the closet door, pull the covers back over my head, and pray that the skeletal specter would disappear.

One night, after months of trying to convince me that there was no skeleton in the closet, my mother concocted a new plan. When she came to tuck me in, my eyes fixed on the closet and she said something that changed my entire view. "Susan, why don't you invite the skeleton to come out and play? Who knows, he may be fun."

What a brilliant move: concede the existence of scary things, and invite them out to play. Apparently, my mom was not the first to think of this approach, as the great Irish playwright George Bernard Shaw once wrote, "If you can't get rid of the skeleton in your closet, you'd best take it out and teach it to dance."

Today, even though there are no more wire hangers or Garanimals in my closet, I still use that same twist of perspective. I have to! The skeletons we fear as adults are at least as big and scary as the ones from our childhood. And those bony creatures can steal your joy in a split second.

Some of us worry about the skeleton of money who rattles his bones every time we hear rumors of layoffs, read about impending recessions, or see towering stacks of bills piling up on our kitchen table. Others tremble at the health skeleton who sends shivers down our spine when we discover yet another person has been diagnosed with cancer. There is the skeleton of shame that hides in the closet of many a heart, constantly threatening to lurch out. And then there are the ugly skeletons of hatred, prejudice, and racism.

The effect of those skeletons on us as adults is exactly the same as it was when we were kids. We feel an overwhelming urge to slam the closet door, pull the covers over our heads, and pray that the bony specter goes away.

This reminds me of a skeleton joke:

Why didn't the skeleton cross the road?

He didn't have the guts.

Okay, I know, I know. Groan. But here's the point: the only way we can get past the paralyzing fear of the skeletons lurking in our hearts is to have the guts to invite them into the light. It is then that the problems fade, change, even transform, and our fears start to subside.

The prophet Ezekiel understood this same struggle when he stood in the valley of lifeless dry bones, but he found the guts to face the bones through the word of God. In that moment of faith, those scary dead bones began to come together, to stand up, and to play and dance in their newfound life (Ezekiel 37).

What's the biggest, baddest skeleton in your closet right now?

What would happen if you found the courage to hold it up to the light?

We all have our scary skeletons. But nothing in our dark closets is stronger than the holy promise made to us of a second chance and a new life. If we can find the guts to invite those bony fears out, then we can be sure that God will make them dance.

Questions to Consider:

-   What scary things are you hiding from?

-   What would that thing look like outside its dark, ominous closet?

-   What if you invited it to dance like Ezekiel's dry bones? What if you offered it a cupcake?

Focus on What Could Go Right

"You can't live a positive life with a negative mind."

- Anonymous

Sometimes the world doesn't steal our joy. Sometimes we simply give it away. Let me give you an example.

The last flight I took before COVID-19 hit was like living through a combination of the movies *Airplane!* (a comedy) and *Airport 1970* (a tragedy). We were traveling from New York to Salt Lake City, and everything seemed fine until we were halfway down the runway, when the plane began to shake violently and the emergency air masks began to drop.

A few tense moments later, the pilot announced, "You probably noticed a little noise and shaking on our takeoff. We blew a tire, and we were too far down the runway to stop. We don't think we have hydraulic damage, so we are going on to Salt Lake in order to burn as much fuel as possible before our landing" (which I took as shorthand for *so as to minimize the explosion on impact*). And then he added my favorite part of the announcement: "Enjoy your flight, and thanks for flying Delta!"

At that point, most people—most normal people, that is—went back to reading their book or taking their nap. But me, oh no. I decide to log into the Gogo Inflight Internet in order to research all the things that could go wrong. Not surprisingly, the first entry was a report on an Air France flight that blew a tire and exploded into flames less than two minutes after takeoff.

Okay, so I went a little crazy. But it was scary, and like many people, my first reaction was to focus on the things that could go wrong. In short, people tend to give our joy away.

Human beings have been worrying about what could go wrong since time began. The worst culprit today? WebMD. Who hasn't searched WebMD for information about something minor like a headache and, in a matter of minutes, determined that you're about to die of an aneurism?

How about this example: you send your boss a project, and she doesn't immediately respond. Instead of thinking that she hasn't answered because she's busy, you immediately jump to the conclusion that she hasn't responded because she hates it and is about to fire you.

Another classic case is when your spouse or partner seems a little quiet, so you immediately decide something is terribly wrong and proceed to ask him or her, "Is everything okay?" every five seconds.

Why do we do this? We don't start this way—we aren't born with an innate skepticism, a tendency to focus on the negative. Sadly, over time, we become conditioned to expect the worst. Think of all the sayings we learn, such as "Hope for the best and expect the worst," or my personal favorite, Murphy's law: "If anything can go wrong, it will."

By the way . . . who is Murphy?

Whoever he is, our mind is conditioned to expect the worst, and the mind is a powerful thing. As the great seventeenth-century poet John Milton wrote, "The mind is its own place, and in itself can make a heaven of hell, and a hell of heaven."

Focusing on what could go wrong is a self-fulfilling prophesy. Compare it to riding a bike: If you look at the ground, you lose your balance and fall to the ground. Likewise, if you obsess about what could go wrong, your consuming fear may contribute to it actually going wrong. If nothing else, you'll make yourself sick . . . which will send you back to WebMD.

It's also a waste of time. When you spend time worrying about what might go wrong in the future, you miss the present—which, by the way, is a present. We have all been given a finite amount of time in this life. Do you want to live it in fear or in joy?

Since I'm here, you obviously know the ending of my airplane story. Eventually, we landed. It was a little harrowing with a lot of shaking and loud noises and a few emergency vehicles, but we made it. And I learned a good lesson.

But then another thought crossed my mind. *What if they lost my luggage?*

Questions to Consider:

- Do you tend to immediately jump to what could go wrong? Why? Were you like that as a child? Where did you get it from?

- Do you spend time with negative people? Do they affect your point of view? (See next chapter.)

- How do you start your day? News? Emails? Social Media? How about a gratitude journal instead?

(Why, yes! I did write one. Thanks for asking. "Grace-Filled Gratitude: A 40 Day Joy Journal with Inspirational Scriptures!" Available on Amazon. ☺)

Love Your Neighbor . . .
Unless Your Neighbor is a Squirrel

"'NO' is a complete sentence."

- Anne Lamott

I am an ordained minister who is expected to teach people to "Love your neighbor."

And I do.

But recently, I found an exception to that rule. Love your neighbor . . . unless your neighbor is a squirrel.

My discovery happened several weeks ago, when my husband, Toby, placed a fresh loaf of sourdough bread on our kitchen counter to cool. We left to run errands, only to return to find a giant hole gnawed through the kitchen screen and my enemy, the squirrel, sitting on the counter. While his eyes conveyed a "Who, me?" look, his bread-stuffed cheeks told the full story. Furious, we chased him around the house until Toby caught him in a fishing net and tossed his furry behind out of our home.

We repaired the screen, but several days later, the same thing happened again. A week later, we installed a "chew-proof" screen, and that afternoon, we discovered my now *arch*enemy, the squirrel, with his head buried in a casserole of mac and cheese cooling on the counter.

Mac and cheese, people.

The book of Revelations 6:8 talks about such things: "And I looked, and behold a pale squirrel . . . and hell followed with him."

Or was it a horse?

Either way. While you may not have a furry creature breaking into your home and eating your mac and cheese and sourdough bread, we all have our squirrels—the things that wiggle their way into our psyche and eat at the good things in our life, the things that devour our sense of joy and well-being before we even have time to taste them.

Maybe it's the squirrel that sits on your shoulder and chatters that you don't have enough money saved, that you might lose your job, or that you might not be able to pay your rent.

Maybe it's the squirrel that burrows its way into every waking moment with worries that the tickle in the back of your throat is an early COVID-19 symptom.

Or maybe it's the worry that your child, or you as a teacher, may have to return to the petri dish of a classroom this fall.

Whatever your squirrels, you must find a way to keep them at bay before they devour everything good and sustaining around you.

My suggestion? Follow our blueprint.

First, do what you can to screen out your squirrels. That may mean turning off the news every once in a while so you can avoid the headlines blaring at you 24/7. It could mean stopping the constant scrolling through social media posts. And it definitely means screening out the negative, judgmental people in our lives. (Can I have an amen?)

It's amazing what a strong screen can do to hold at bay the things that gnaw away at our happiness.

But as Toby and I found out, squirrels can still get through even the strongest screens. That's when you need a strong hand to toss them out of your house.

One such hand is a strong sense of self. Loving your neighbor doesn't mean loving someone or something to the point of your own destruction. It doesn't mean leaving your windows open so that the world can come in and eat away at your happiness. Remember, the commandment "Love your neighbor" came with a crucial counterbalance: Love your neighbor . . . as yourself.

While personal boundaries are important, Psalm 34:4 shares the most powerful hand we can find: "I sought the Lord, and he answered me and delivered me from all my fears." God is the only one who knows all the nooks and crannies where those pesky squirrels can hide. All we have to do is acknowledge our fear and ask for help. Then God will usher out the most troublesome invaders.

The moral of the story? Protect the good things in your life. Screen out your squirrels. And when the screen can't hold, find a strong hand to toss them out. You are worthy of joy, and as a child of God, you have the right to all the mac and cheese life has to offer.

Questions to Consider:

- What things are wiggling their way into your mental household and devouring your sense of happiness and well-being?

- What kind of screens can you put in place to keep them out?

- What power can you access to throw them out of your house?

The Long Way Around

"Our patience will achieve more than our force."

- Edmund Burke, *Irish statesman*

I have decided that New York City is the best place to live if you want to take the long way around. Recently, I had to take four detours in order to get home. The first was on Park Avenue, where police were sending everyone north because of construction. We turned again because of a parade, and then we took another detour due to a street fair. Finally, traffic came to a stop when a man chose to rant about the issues of the day in the middle of Third Avenue.

And so it goes in our fair city. You're trying to go one way, but thanks to construction, a parade, or a man ranting in the middle of Third Avenue, you have to take the long way around.

We've all been there, perhaps in more ways than one.

Perhaps you're in a relationship that seems to be taking the long way around. Maybe your career path is unfolding with unwelcome twists and turns. Or perhaps injury has forced a delay in your life. It's frustrating when these things happen. But as frustrating as it is, taking the long way may be the best thing that can happen to us.

Thousands of years ago, God led the Israelites the long way around: "When Pharaoh let the people go, God did not lead them by way of the land of the Philistines, although that was nearer"

(Exodus 13:17). But God had a reason: "For God said, 'If the people face war, they may change their minds and return to Egypt.' So God led the people by the roundabout way of the wilderness toward the Red Sea" (Exodus 13:17-18).

God knew the Israelites—their fears, their hopes, and their capabilities—and designated a route based on what they could do. It may not have been the fastest route. In fact, it was a roundabout way through the wilderness. But it was a route that took them away from dangers and threats that would have thrown them off their quest. Long as it was, it was still a path that would get them to the promised land.

That's a lesson we all need. Sometimes the long way around is the best way because we're not ready for the direct route. In fact, the long way around may be the quickest way to joy.

Think about it like this . . .

What if you found your dream job but hadn't fully developed the right skill set? What if you discovered the perfect relationship, yet lacked the emotional bandwidth to nurture it? What if a great opportunity presented itself when you didn't have the depth or grounding to step into it?

Sometimes we need time to mature into our best selves before we start down the fast track.

We can see the same principle at work in nature. For example, consider the growth cycle of Chinese bamboo. It grows only about two inches a year for the first four years. Then, if nurtured correctly, it grows up to eighty feet in the fifth year. It takes time in those beginning years to generate a sufficient root system to support the exponential growth at the end.

Where in your life do you feel you are taking the long way around?

Why do you think you've been led that way?

It's hard when we feel we are not on the fast track. We worry about being delayed. We fret over arriving late. But late on whose schedule?

Our timetable is not the one that matters. What matters is the timeline God has placed in front of each of us. We can choose to fight it. Or we can trust the process, knowing that long way or not, God will eventually lead us home.

Questions to Consider:

- Where in your life do you feel you are on the long way around?

- Why do you believe you are on this path?

- What joyful plans might God have for you on this longer route?

Put on Your Mask . . . and Smize!

"Smile. It's the boldest statement you can
make without saying a word."

- Anonymous

Going to the grocery store these days makes me feel like I'm one of
the astronaut characters in the movie *The Martian*. Just this
morning, my husband and I made our once-every-two-weeks early-
morning trip to the Fairway Market on Second Avenue and 30th
Street in New York City. Donning masks and rubber gloves, we left
our apartment with two backpacks, a rolling cart, and several
container bags, as if we were preparing for an interplanetary mission.

Of course, everyone else who was out and about on their own
Mars mission was wearing a mask too, but this morning, we noticed
something different. While most people kept a fairly flat facial
expression behind their mask as they passed, one young woman
looked up and smiled. Instinctively, both my husband and I smiled
back at her.

How do I know she smiled? Because she smized.

For those of you who are not fans of the television show
America's Next Top Model, "smize" is slang for "smiling with your
eyes." First coined by the host of the show, supermodel Tyra Banks,
"smize" combines the word *smile* with the sound of the word *eyes*.

In these days of COVID-19 and the new era of masks, what could be more important than to smize?

Smiling (or smizing, these days) can transform our entire outlook. Psychologists and scientists as far back as Charles Darwin have argued that emotions can be regulated by behavior. We usually think the opposite—that we smile when we are feeling happy—but science has shown that we can create happiness by the act of forming a smile.

For example, scientists have discovered that when a person smiles, it triggers physiological changes in the brain that cool the blood, which in turn controls our mood, which causes a feeling of happiness. Translation: we can change our inward emotion by changing our outward expression.

And that's just the beginning. What we feel in our hearts manifests itself in our behavior, and how we act over time is what we become. Consistently reminding ourselves to smile throughout our daily lives may eventually change our hearts. And when our hearts change, the way we encounter the world changes. That is when we can truly begin to affect those around us.

I think of the famous lyrics by Louis Armstrong: "When you're smiling, the whole world smiles with you." Armstrong was onto something, as neuroscience has shown that merely seeing a smile (or a frown) activates mirror neurons in the brain that mimic the other person's emotion. Translation: When someone smiles at us, we smile back, and vice versa. And now, thanks to my empirical research on the way to the grocery store, we know that seeing a smile expressed through the eyes has the exact same effect.

This idea has caught on in a number of industries, including the hospitality business. For example, both Walt Disney World and the

Ritz Carlton use what's called the 10/5 Rule. When hotel employees are within ten feet of a guest, they must make eye contact and smile. When they get within five feet of the guest, they must say hello. The bottom line? Joy is contagious.

Here's the moral of the story: Just because you are wearing a mask and feeling like you are on a Mars mission doesn't mean you can't feel and share joy. In fact, this is a time when we need joy more than ever!

Try it this week. Put on your mask and smize! As my dear friend Rabbi Bob Alper once said, "When we are called to our maker, we will each be held responsible for all the opportunities for joy that we ignored."

Questions to Consider:

- What opportunities for joy have you ignored recently?

- Have you noticed anyone "smizing" at you through a mask? How did you feel?

- Try "smizing" at least once. And do it today! See what reactions you get.

A TIARA

"Oh, It's Just You!"

"Not knowing something doesn't make you a fraud.
It makes you a student."

- Marie Forleo, *author*

One of my best Halloween outfits when I was little was a gypsy zombie. It was all homemade with "Heinz Ketchup blood" smeared on my face, my mom's scarf tied around my head, some giant clip-on earrings that we found at a yard sale, and a flowy paisley housecoat. I have no clue where the idea for that wacky concoction originated. What I do remember is that I knew (at least in my young mind) that I looked terribly scary.

Apparently, I was the only one who thought so. Trick-or-treating bag in hand, I proceeded next door to terrify my eight-year-old neighbor. As he opened his front door, he rolled his eyes and said, "Oh, it's just you."

Maybe it was the disappointment of being called out, or the shame of not being considered scary. Whatever it was, that moment stuck with me for years. It stole my tiara.

Sadly, the "Oh, it's just you" fear is still alive and well in many of us. Self-help gurus have renamed it imposter syndrome: the fear that the world is going to find out that you're a fake, that you don't belong, or that you aren't as smart, or as successful, or as good as everyone seems to think. The anxiety is that if we show our true selves, the world will roll its eyes and say, "Oh, it's just you!"

To protect ourselves from this painful revelation, we create emotional masks. They are not so different from the masks that the ancient Celts created to protect themselves from the evil spirits that roamed the earth on All Hallows' Eve. We, too, don our emotional masks to protect ourselves from the judgmental people who roam our lives.

For example, if we are insecure, we might hide behind the mask of name-dropping. If we are unsure of our power, we might wear the mask of being a bully. If we don't think the world loves us, we might hold up the mask of anger.

The problem is that it's exhausting to live such an inauthentic life. You put on a mask or two or ten, then take off a few, then put on a couple more. Who has the energy for that? Worst of all, you forget who you really are. As comedian and actress Fanny Brice once explained, "Let the world know you as you are, not as you think you should be, because sooner or later, if you are posing, you will forget the pose, and then, where are you?"

We weren't born with masks. We put them on, therefore we can take them off. Start with this simple exercise: Think about a negative message about yourself that you are trying to mask. Is it true? More than likely, the answer is no. And if it is not true, then ask yourself, "Why am I continuing to hold on to that message? If I stopped believing it, what would happen?"

One of the main risks we face in taking off our mask is the world's reaction. Opening yourself up can threaten others because it pushes them to reevaluate their own lives. Many times, it forces them to realize that they, too, have the power to change, but they haven't done it.

Don't let that stop you. Your life, your voice, and your spirit are gifts from God. The Psalmists acknowledge this truth with the beautiful words, "I am fearfully and wonderfully made" (Psalm 139:14). Our gifts need to be shared, not masked. Or, as a pastor colleague once said: "Masks make shallow what God has intended to be deep."

Think about the masks you wear and why. Commit to taking the mask off and putting your God-given tiara on. Shine your gifts out to the world—no apology, no shame, no regrets. And if someone says, "Oh, it's just you," smile and know without reservation that being "you" is more than enough.

Questions to Consider:

- Do you ever worry that the world will find you out?

- What masks do you wear? What negative messages about yourself have you chosen to believe?

- What would happen if you took off your masks and brought all of who you are to what you do? What would you look like, sounds like, and act like if you were proudly wearing your tiara?

Life Lessons from a Dogsled Team

"Alone we can do so little. Together we can do so much."

- Helen Keller

Years ago, during the innocence (and ignorance) of my youth, I signed up for an Outward Bound dog-sledding trip in the Boundary Waters of northern Minnesota near the Canadian Border.

In January.

Oh, and we were camping.

It was there that I spent ten of the coldest days of my life learning to run a dogsled team. But this was not your average team of cute huskies you see at the pet shop. The Outward Bound camp had adopted a group of specially bred huskies from the Mawson research outpost in Antarctica. Unlike their stateside brethren, my dogs, including my two leads, Cardiff and Bear, resembled a cross between a miniature pony and a wooly mammoth.

They say what doesn't kill you makes you stronger. To be honest, there were days on that trip when I wasn't sure which it would be. But I lived and eventually made it back to New York City armed with unforgettable life lessons, mostly from the dogs.

Perhaps the most powerful lesson was about life itself—and how to lead it. Those burly dogs wanted nothing more than to pull that sled. It was an ingrained passion. You'd hitch them up and their eyes would light up. Their ears would perk, and they'd be ready to bust out of their harnesses with joy.

Each dog knew its role and had its place. For every team, there were two lead dogs that were particularly skilled at obeying directional commands and finding trails. Behind them were the two point dogs that acted as backup leaders. Directly in front of the sled were the wheel dogs that helped keep the sled on the trail. And in between were the team dogs that brought the power and endurance to keep the sled going.

The success of the team depended on each dog using its particular skill in concert with the others. When they were in full swing, each dog fully zoned into his or her role, it was a thing of grace and beauty. In those moments, I learned the value of using individual strengths to support a group's effort and the lesson that everyone's gifts are important, even if they are different than ours.

Sadly, there were a few dogs at the camp that were injured and unable to pull a full sled. I would spend a little time sitting with one of my favorites every day. Petting her, I couldn't help but notice that her coat and eyes had grown a bit dull. Then, one day, an instructor brought over a tiny, super-light sled that they were going to let her start pulling for a few minutes a day, and she exploded into life.

We all have that place where we, too, come to life—where we feel like we're doing what we were born to do. Of course, there is the opposite as well—the places in life where our coats and our eyes grow dull. And what a waste it is to spend time there.

There's an old saying that every creature has its rightful place, and in that place, it becomes beautiful. The Psalmists put it another way: "I praise you because I am fearfully and wonderfully made"

(Psalm 139:14). Either way, it's an affirmation of our unique gifts and our innate worth in this life.

This week check out this clip from National Geographic (https://www.youtube.com/watch?v=6nVfFNbxX7s) and watch a few minutes of a dogsled team running in the wild to see first-hand the raw passion of those dogs.

Once you see it, you'll never forget. And, perhaps, like me, that image will inspire you to live to your fullest potential and never let your eyes grow dull.

Questions to Consider:

- In what part of your life have your coat and eyes grown dull?

- Where is your rightful place?

- Where is your role on the "team"?

Breast Cancer and the "F" Bomb

"Faith is what you do between the last time you
experienced God and the next time you experience God."

- Renita J. Weems, *Professor of Old Testament*

"Brace yourselves. I'm gunna use the 'F' word to talk about my battle
with breast cancer."

While the audience gasped, the speaker, a slight, scrappy blonde,
smiled. She knew the impact of her words. Pausing with perfect
comedic timing, she then, as promised, dropped her "F" bomb:

"Faith."

And so began Celebration of Life, a breast cancer survivor event
in Watertown, South Dakota. As a survivor myself, I had been
invited as the featured speaker, but the words spoken by Colita, a
stage two survivor and the founder of the local support group, were
what everyone remembered.

Faith is the key.

But let me be clear. Do I mean faith that God will let me live
through a cancer diagnosis?

No.

And none of the survivors I met last week understood faith that
way, either. In fact, not one person there uttered a word of

questioning or judgment about WHY God let this happen or WHY God allows suffering. These women didn't have time for that. They were too busy fighting for their recovery and, most of all, fighting for each other.

For them, and for me, "faith" means a belief that you are not alone, that you have a greater power walking with you and beside you. In fact, one of the survivors at the gathering said to me, "I don't look to God as the source of my pain. I look to God as the source of my healing."

Thousands of years earlier, the Psalmists wrote nearly the same thing: "Yea, though I walk through the valley of the shadow of death, I will fear no evil: for thou art with me; thy rod and thy staff they comfort me" (Psalm 23:4).

Even with such powerful assurances, it's still hard to have faith during our times of crisis. For example, Colita talked about another "F" bomb: fear—the fear that set in when she first heard her diagnosis. Everyone in that room understood what she meant. Whether it's rooted in breast cancer or some other crisis in life, we all know about the power of fear. It seeps into our psyche and changes our perspective on what is possible. It makes us doubt our capabilities. It destroys our tiara.

But faith can reverse that process. Silent screen actress Dorothy Bernard once said, "Courage is fear that has said its prayers." When we pray, we take our focus off ourselves and lock on to the holy power that surrounds us all. It's then that our fear shrinks, our courage roars back, and we muster our reserves to fight. As Colita so artfully said, "It takes faith to bring the fight."

And all of us must fight. We must fight to live well each day we are given. We must fight to appreciate the gift of every moment we have. Some days we must fight for our very lives. But even in the heat of those personal battles, we must also remember to fight for each other.

Some of the survivors gave examples of that kind of fight—kindnesses offered them, such as when someone showed up at their door with a casserole to feed their family, a friend drove them to a treatment ninety miles away, or a neighbor organized care for their children. Just as we have received God's protective presence through faith, we must turn and channel that healing to others.

Colita was right. The "F word" is the best way to approach a cancer diagnosis, or any crisis in this life. Faith reminds us what is important, who is in charge, and why we are here. Faith is what brings the fight. And with God on our side, that's a fight we will never lose. As Psalm 23 promises, surely goodness and mercy shall follow *us* all the days of our lives: and we will dwell in the house of the Lord forever.

Questions to Consider:

- Have you ever blamed God for a difficulty or loss in your life?

- Do you look to God as a source of your pain or a source of your healing?

- Are you walking in faith or fear? Do you feel God walking with you?

Grace Bats Last

"I said I'm going to hit the next one right over the flagpole.
God must have been with me."

- Babe Ruth

I believe in the church of baseball.

Okay, yeah, I stole that line from the opening of the movie *Bull Durham*, but I'm not the only one who has said it or believes it. The novelist F. Scott Fitzgerald called baseball "the faith of fifty million people."

The idea is not that far off. If we look closely, there are helpful parallels between the sport of baseball and the spiritual path. Given the nature of our times, I'd say we could use help anywhere we can find it.

For example, in baseball and in life, there will always be a jeering crowd—people who love to scream judgment and ridicule, who would rather destroy than delight in something great, who revel in stealing tiaras. I'm reminded of this old saying: "Beware of the masses, for sometimes the 'm' falls off."

Babe Ruth experienced that when he stepped up to the plate in game three of the 1932 World Series. The Chicago crowd went crazy, yelling insults and even throwing lemons onto the field. Standing in the batter's box and taking the full force of the insults,

Babe suddenly called for a timeout. He stepped out of the box and pointed his bat toward center field, as if he were calling his shot—as if he were saying to everyone there, "Nothing you can do can touch me."

After a moment, he stepped back in the box, and the pitcher, Charles Root, wound up and flung his best curveball at him. Babe connected with an earthquake-like crack, and the ball soared deep into center field, just where he had predicted. It was the longest home run in Wrigley Field history.

The lesson? Never let the crowd bully you into believing you are less than you are. As Isaiah 43:1 reminds us, "I have called you by your name; you are mine."

Another spiritual lesson from baseball is that we do not play alone. We always have a team surrounding us, even though sometimes we don't see them.

It's like the story about Yankees broadcaster Phil Rizzuto. One day, his colleague looked at Phil's scorecard in the booth and saw "WW"—a notation he didn't recognize. He asked Phil, "What is this?" And Phil replied, "Oh, 'wasn't watching.'"

When you aren't watching, it can feel like you are all alone at the plate. However, if you step back and look at the whole field, you will see the team surrounding you. As Psalm 91:11 says, "For he will command his angels concerning you to guard you in all your ways."

The author Anne Lamott inspires a third spiritual lesson from baseball with her words, "Grace bats last." In baseball lingo, people would say, "Grace bats cleanup." The cleanup batter is always the fourth one in the lineup. The aim is to get the first three batters on base; then, with the bases loaded, the strongest hitter steps up.

We all know that feeling of working and sweating but ultimately reaching the point at which we can do no more. The crowd is jeering. We feel alone. We are being pitched nothing but curve balls and sliders. Nothing short of a miracle will do.

In that moment, we must have faith that the strongest hitter—grace—will step in and bring us safely home. As Matthew 19:26 tells us, "With God all things are possible."

Yes, I believe in the church of baseball. I believe in all of God's houses—sports, spiritual, or otherwise. Each offers us lessons that can help us through. So, the next time you're surrounded by doubters and the bases are loaded, remember that the jeering crowd can't touch you.

You are part of a team for which grace bats last.

Questions to Consider:

- Where do you hear the jeering crowds?

- When do you feel most alone?

- What miracle do you await?

Smoking in the Shower

"We judge people in areas where we're
vulnerable to shame."

- Brené Brown

I love smoking in the shower.

Not literally, or at least not in the way you might be thinking. I love "smoking in the shower," which is the name my favorite diner gives to smoked salmon on a bagel. I don't eat it often—only as a treat, and usually while alone in my apartment so I don't have to share. Basically, the same way one would sneak a cigarette while hiding in the bathroom.

We all have our "smoking in the shower" moments: the things we do when no one is looking; the things that may feel good at the time but in the long run don't make us stronger.

Like chowing down on a giant container of Ben and Jerry's in secret.

Or binge-watching angry talk shows into the wee hours of the morning.

Or managing up at work. We all know people who are super-attentive and polite to their bosses but difficult and disrespectful to their subordinates when the higher-ups aren't looking.

How about posting vicious social media posts and hiding behind anonymity?

Or saying judgmental, ugly, or racist things when no one else of that color, ethnicity, or religion is around?

"Smoking in the shower" moments happens in all aspects of life. But here's the thing we have to remember: Over time, what we do in private drives who we are in public.

It could be as basic as what we eat or drink in private. Ten years ago, I did a cross-country drive from New York to Alaska. Trying to do it on the cheap, I ate a lot of McDonald's and bought low-quality gas. It caught up with me somewhere in the Yukon when my Jeep could barely climb a hill and I couldn't fit in my overalls. If we abuse our bodies in private, we're eventually going to give out in public.

It could also be what we feed our minds. If we spend our time in private filling our minds with negative, destructive things, then in public, we are going to speak and act on those harmful forces. In short, what goes in comes out. Not unlike garlic. If you eat it for dinner, you will share it with everyone you encounter.

In the end, what we do in private forms our foundation. It drives how we think, what we think about, and how we engage others. If our foundation is strong, our words, our work, and our purpose are grounded in value and significance. If, however, we draw on those negative forces, like road salt on a car frame, our foundation will corrode.

Here's the good news: No matter what choices we have made in the past, no matter how many times we have found ourselves smoking in the shower, we can change. And here's the double good news: We don't have to do it alone. There's a little something called prayer that can clean our deepest corrosion. As Mother Teresa said, "Prayer changes us, and we change things."

Prayer is actually the opposite of smoking in the shower. It is something we can do when no one is looking that makes us feel good AND makes us stronger. (It also has fewer calories than a bagel slathered with cream cheese and smoked salmon.)

Don't let your choices in private corrode who you are in public. Don't destroy your own tiara.

Dig your foundations deep. Build your life on worthy, noble virtues. Make your stand on the rock of prayer. As Henry David Thoreau wrote, "If you've built castles in the air, your work need not be lost. That's where they should be. Now put foundations under them."

Questions to Consider:

- What were your recent "smoking in the shower" moments?

- Have they affected how you treated yourself, or engaged others?

- How is your prayer life?

The Magic of Chicken Poop

"The person who doesn't make mistakes
doesn't make anything."

- Anonymous

Have you ever made a mistake?

If no, then please stop reading and head to the sports or weather section.

If, on the other hand, you are like us other human beings, and have made a slip or two, stay with me.

Three things are sure in this life: death, taxes, and mistakes. We all make mistakes. Like the time I wrote a column on Elvis and said that his birthplace was Memphis, Tennessee.

Nope.

Tupelo, Mississippi. That's about a 110-mile mistake. (Oops!)

The question is whether we use these slip-ups as an excuse or as an experience to grow.

I am reminded of my grandmother, Emma Sue Whitmire, who had a beautiful garden on her farm near Asheville in the North Carolina mountains. There she grew the biggest, *Jurassic Park*-sized tomatoes I'd ever seen. I asked her one day how she did it.

"Chicken poop," she said dryly. "A garden won't grow right without it."

It took a few years before I enjoyed a tomato out of her garden again. But I never forgot the lesson: It's the messy, unpleasant stuff that grows a great garden. Just like sometimes it's the messy stuff in life—the mistakes and wrong turns—that grow a rich existence.

Yet we bemoan every tiny mistake. We begin to define ourselves by the wrong turns. Over time, the shine on our tiara begins to dim.

I think of my first Good Friday service as a newly ordained pastor. I was so nervous that I accidentally spliced the words to the Lord's Prayer and the 23rd Psalm.

"Lead us not into . . . *um* . . . the valley . . . of the shadow of death? Because . . . *um* . . . it's a bad place—that valley. Thank you? Forever and ever amen."

Needless to say, there were some confused looks as the congregation raised their heads after the prayer. For the rest of the time, I sat behind the pulpit contemplating what other careers I might pursue. As the service ended, one of our senior members came up to me and said, "Well, I've never heard the Lord's Prayer done that way, but it sure made me sit up and listen!" You never know what growth and learning will come from a mistake.

Then there are the times that your "slip-up" may not even be a mistake. The world is threatened by things it doesn't understand. Many times innovation is labeled as a mistake. For example, in 1954, early in Elvis's career, the manager of the Grand Ole Opry fired him after just one performance, telling *him*, "You ain't goin' nowhere, son." What a tragedy if Elvis had taken that criticism as truth and walked away from his music.

Elvis wasn't the only one. J. K. Rowling had her Harry Potter series rejected by twelve publishers before it made her a billionaire. Steven Spielberg was rejected from the University of Southern California School of Theater, Film, and Television three times. And Johann Sebastian Bach was the third choice for organist at the Saint Thomas Church in Leipzig.

If you are handwringing over a recent mistake, ask yourself two questions: Was it really a mistake—like Memphis versus Tupelo? Or was it the world being threatened by something new? Either way, it can feel like chicken poop.

But that's not the end of the story. Find a way to use that mistake, that criticism, that messy, unpleasant stuff of life to grow. Who knows? In the end, you may find yourself cultivating a bountiful garden.

Questions to Consider:

- What recent mistake have you made?

- Did you beat yourself up over it? Why?

- What wonderful new thing can you grow from that "poop"?

Sinners at the Laundromat

"Shame occurs when you haven't been able to get away with the 'who' you want people to think you are."

- Carl Whitaker, *pioneer family therapist*

While on vacation one summer, while all good Christians were congregating in church, all evil sinners (including me and my husband, Toby) were congregating in the laundromat.

I thought we were safe until somewhere mid–spin cycle when a scarily clean-shaven gentleman walked into the laundromat and said, "A blessed morning to you, brothers and sisters" (a warning sign, if ever there was one).

I could see he had a number of brochures in his hand, but I tried my best not to make eye contact. Sure enough, he came to me first. I think it was because of the T-shirt I was wearing that read: "Lead me not into temptation, I can find it myself."

"Sister," he asked in the most earnest of tones, "have you met Jesus?"

Not wanting to get into a whole thing about how I was an ordained Baptist minister on vacation in Wisconsin skipping church because I wasn't Lutheran and, more importantly, was planning to go pan fishing instead, I simply said, "No sir, I haven't seen hide nor hair of Jesus this morning."

He then handed me a tract with a picture of Jesus holding a tiny lamb that was looking a bit queasy, and said, "You know, Jesus can wash your sins away better than any of these machines." And with that, he went to the sinner next to me at the industrial-sized dryer and started his pitch again.

Later, I thought about my new friend and his earnest attempts to save us. Was there a lesson here? Spiritual laundry, perhaps?

Consider the three categories of dirty clothes. First, things that don't need to be washed. If you are like me, you tend to occasionally leave clothes on the floor that aren't dirty—clothes you can put right back on and wear with pride.

Similarly, there are things in our lives that don't need cleaning, like our physical traits (signs of aging included), our ethnicities, our race, and our gender. These are gifts from God that do not need to be washed; they need to be celebrated and worn with pride to celebrate our maker. As Psalm 139 tells us, "For you created my inmost being; you knit me together in my mother's womb. I praise you because I am fearfully and wonderfully made."

Then there is the second category of laundry, which just needs the delicate cycle with the least agitation. In the washing machine, these would be things like silk or polyester. In life, these would be things like mistakes, hurt feelings, or use of colorful language because you couldn't get into your jeans that morning.

Don't waste time getting agitated over this stuff. Use a short and delicate wash cycle. Acknowledge that you're wrong; say you're sorry and move on. And do it now. If you wait, delicate stains can become hard to get out.

Which brings us to category three: the industrial-strength stuff. These are the heavy stains that have been ground-in over time. Things like anger, shame, resentment, and self-loathing.

The only thing we can do with this nasty pile of laundry is to get ourselves an industrial-strength spot remover—a spiritual OxiClean, something or someone that will go deep into those buried places and release the stains.

Again, the Psalmists have the answer. "As far as the east is from the west, so far has he removed our transgressions from us" (Psalm 103:12). When we allow God to work—when we accept God's forgiveness—something profound happens. The stains start to break up, we begin to forgive ourselves, and we walk back into the world clean and fresh, ready for the work ahead.

The next time you are doing laundry, ask yourself three questions: What in my life does not need washing? What in my life just needs a delicate cleaning? What in my life needs an industrial-strength stain remover?

Do a little spiritual laundry. In the end, it will all come out in the wash.

Questions to Consider:

- What in my life does not need washing?

- What in my life just needs a delicate cleaning?

- What in my life needs an industrial-strength stain remover?

Lose the Training Wheels

"Keep the shiny side up and the rubber side down."

- Biker slogan

I bought my first motorcycle in the spring of 1995. A used black Harley Sportster 883, all chromed up, with snakeskin fringe on the handlebars and wicked custom pipes. It was love at first sight. The perfect match. And we were together exactly one hour and seventeen minutes.

I had just gotten my motorcycle license the day before on a Honda Rebel (with about one-fourth of the Sportster's engine power and one-half the weight). The sane thing would have been to buy a Rebel, spend some road time on it, and then think about graduating to a bigger bike. But that's not how I roll.

The first one hour and sixteen minutes of my relationship with the new Harley were taken up by signing the papers at the dealership. The seventeenth and last minute we were together was spent riding across the street from the dealership and into a parking lot, where I promptly crashed into a guardrail in front of a passing police car.

As if the sting from that wasn't enough, the officer, after helping me bring the bike upright, said with a smirk, "Maybe you'd better keep the training wheels on a bit longer."

Ouch.

Unfortunately, I took those words straight to heart and didn't get back on a bike for years. The excuses kept rolling around in my head:

"I can't get back on. He's probably right; I have no business riding."

"I can't get back on; I might fall and really get hurt this time."

"I can't get back on; I just need a little more time."

Biker or not, we all have our training wheels: the excuses we use when we don't want to move out of our comfort zone.

It's easier to live life with training wheels. It's less scary. It's less threatening. But life with training wheels is also less meaningful. It's like Edgar Lee Masters wrote in the poem "The George Gray": "It is a boat longing for the sea, and yet afraid."

That said, we can find many an excuse to justify our training wheels. Like what other people think. At one time or another, we've all been the target of unkind words. Sadly, we tend to let those words sink in and take root. Soon your heart is overgrown with doubt. Our tiara begins to slip. The lesson? Never let the world tell you what is possible. Just remember that those who discourage your dreams probably do so because they had their own dreams destroyed.

Is your excuse that you might fall or fail? Three things are sure in this life: death, taxes, and mistakes. They are going to happen. We simply need to change our perspective. For example, when asked how it felt to fail so many times in trying to invent the light bulb, Thomas Edison replied, "I never failed once. It just happened to be a two-thousand-step process."

Are you using the excuse of time? "Oh, I'm not quite ready; I just need a little more time." While, on its face, this doesn't appear to be an excuse, in reality, it's the most dangerous one of all. We delay until the "right time" (which, by the way, doesn't exist) and eventually we completely forget the dream.

My first memory of training wheels is from learning to ride a tiny Schwinn bicycle as a child. When my dad finally suggested we take off the training wheels, I offered all manner of excuses. He simply listened, smiled, and said, "No … it's time."

Ten years after my wreck, I finally got back on a bike. But I started with baby steps: a small Honda Rebel, then a larger bike, and then finally another Harley Sportster. It was scary, it was daunting, but it was time.

What opportunities and dreams are unfolding on the path in front of you? And what training wheels are you leaning on?

Don't waste your life on excuses. Don't miss the opportunities offered. Lose the training wheels, get out on the open road of life, and see what adventures await!

Questions to Consider:

- Where have you fallen and not gotten up?

- What excuses did you use to stay down?

- What opportunities are you missing by not moving forward?

LOVE

The Time Is Ripe for Miracles

"Miracles are a retelling in small letters of the very
same story which is written across the whole world
in letters too large for some of us to see."

– C. S. Lewis, *British writer and theologian*

Now that we have claimed our cupcakes and are proudly wearing our tiaras, we must harness that power for love, healing, even miracles! Yet, as soon as I say that word, "miracle," I know many people will immediately roll their eyes.

I'm afraid that miracles have gotten a bad name. Part of the problem is a regrettable subset of my clergy profession known as TV evangelists. You know the kind . . . folks with large, blow-dried white hair who holler, "Just touch the television screen and shout, 'Thank You, Jesus!' Then mail a check for $49.95, and your psoriasis will be healed!"

The trashy rags you see in the grocery store check-out line also cast shade on the idea of miracles. The last one I saw featured this headline: "Cactus in Arizona Grows in Exact Shape of Gathering at Last Supper!"

Then there's the worst culprit of all: our own doubt. Nurtured by years of disappointments, we begin to believe that miracles aren't possible—or at least not for us.

How tragic. Deeply embedded under our unhealed psoriasis, unrealized communion cactus, and unhinged confidence, I believe that there lies a tiny ember of hope that maybe, just maybe, miracles may still be possible. In fact, times like these—times of upheaval and difficulty—are ripe for miracles.

The Celts called tumultuous times of change "thin places." Others, such as Franciscan father and author Richard Rohr, call them liminal spaces, those places "betwixt and between the familiar and the completely unknown" where fresh new growth can emerge. Rohr explains the significance of such places as "the realm where God can best get at us because our false certitudes are finally out of the way.... The threshold is God's waiting room ... an appointment with the divine Doctor."

If our world has ever been in a liminal space, it's now. If we as a people have ever been in a liminal space, it's now. Truly, it is a time ripe for miracles.

Unfortunately, this is the point at which things usually break down. We read words like this, get our hopes up—again—and then sit back and wait for a miracle to happen. The operative word being "wait." What we fail to realize is that we have agency in those miracles.

Think about all the miracles written about in the Bible. God created the miracle of manna, but the Israelites had to go out and gather it each day. At the wedding in Cana, Jesus commanded the stewards to fill up the stone jars with water. As they poured, the water turned into wine. Heaven provided the miracle; humans provided the means of delivery.

Recently, I read a story about Ashley Richer, a photographer who donates Disney-themed photo shoots to children with cancer.

Ashley lost a young family friend to cancer. Rather than "wait" for future miracles to happen, she decided to use her God-given gifts, her miracles, to make dreams come true.

One such dream happened for five-year-old Arianna Taft. While Arianna was fighting a rare form of kidney cancer, Ashley invited her to do a photo shoot, complete with costumes, special effects, and backgrounds. Soon Arianna was transformed into Snow White, Elsa from *Frozen*, and Merida from *Brave*. A heavenly miracle of joy and hope was brought to fruition through humble human hands.

There are miracles all around us waiting to happen—waiting for us to make them happen. And Lord knows, we could sure use some. Like little Arianna, we do not know what tomorrow will bring, but we do know who holds tomorrow. And that's all that truly matters. For in that liminal place of turbulence and transition, all things, including miracles, are possible.

Questions to Consider:

- Who in your life needs a miracle?

- What in your community, your nation, or your world needs a miracle?

- What abilities and gifts do you have that can usher in those miracles?

Sarah's Purse

I always knew it would be a great day when Sarah Goodson walked through the door of our church carrying her big purse. Raised during the Depression on a sharecropper's farm in the South Carolina Lowcountry, Sarah loved two things in this life more than anything: her family and taking care of others. She moved to New York City in the 1940s to give her family a better life, and she became a nurse in order to care for others.

She shaped her life around making those two things a priority, including what she carried in her purse.

I'm not going to kid you, I love all my congregation, but I especially loved to see Sarah coming in with her big ole purse. That's because I knew what was in it. After each service, she would open that overstuffed pocketbook and pull out the newest photos of her grandkids (not individual photos, but books of photos). Then, as the picture albums were being passed around, little Ziploc bags and Tupperware containers would magically emerge from that purse— bags full of fried chicken, collard greens, shrimp and okra gumbo, oxtail stew, hot corn muffins with blueberries, and, of course, peanut butter pie.

One time I asked Sarah how she got all that stuff in her purse, and she told me about a ritual she performed every Saturday night. She would sit at her kitchen table, remove all the extra, heavy junk in her bag that she had collected during the week, then fill it back up with the important things: photos of her grandkids and food to feed her church.

It was a simple thing, cleaning out a purse. Yet it had such an impact—the smiles on people's faces as they looked at the photos of the grandchildren and the comfort felt by all who ate that delicious food made with pure love.

Perhaps we should all do a little Saturday night purse cleaning of our own hearts. Let's start with this question: What baggage are you carrying today that you should unload? In short, what is keeping you from loving fully?

Everyone's answer is different. Maybe it's resentments or jealousies. Maybe it's an old emotional wound that just won't heal. Or maybe it's that we don't believe we deserve to love and be loved.

But we have an alternative. Even if we don't know how to clean out our own hearts, we can hand our baggage to a greater power. As Jesus said, "Come to me all ye who are heavy laden, and I will give you rest" (Matthew 11:28).

This leads to my next question: What will you put in the place of this baggage? What is important to you? For what purpose are you here?

I suggest that we follow Sarah's lead in this, too. When I had the great honor of performing Sarah's funeral after she passed away several years ago, the message that people shared over and over was that she had brought them joy and made them feel loved.

Is there any greater legacy?

This week, I invite you to do a Saturday night purse cleaning in your life. Identify the things that are weighing you down emotionally, physically, or spiritually. Let them go. Then take your newfound time and energy and focus it on the things that are important. Spend time with your family. Share photographs that make people smile. Stuff a Ziploc bag of yummy food in your purse or pocket and share it with others.

Bring a little love to this hungry world. And do it today. Life is too hard and too short to carry things that just don't matter.

Questions to Consider:

- What things are you carrying in your emotional purse that weigh you down?

- If you could clean it out, what new things would you put in?

Justifying Mac and Cheese Hotdogs

"Hell has three gates: Lust, anger, and greed."

– The Bhagavad Gita

Think about the last time you went shopping. When you got to the checkout counter, how many of the items in your cart did you actually need? Not all of them, I bet.

I, too, am guilty of buying items that aren't exactly necessary. The last time I was at our cabin in Wisconsin, I visited a local butcher whose shop is known for its beautiful meat and creative flavorings. Intending only to purchase hamburger meat for our cookout, I was waylaid by a sign near the checkout counter that for me was like Odysseus's sirens calling from the rocks (of the freezer section): "Mac and Cheese Hotdogs! A gooey favorite stuffed inside a premium wiener. Pasta and cheddar may ooze out while grilling."

Four words rang in my head: Can't. Live. Without. It.

Were these outrageous hotdogs absolutely necessary for my health and well-being?

Yes.

Okay, no. But clearly, the line between what I truly needed and what I simply wanted had become blurred.

Honestly, what do we really need beyond food, water, clothing, and shelter? And please understand that by food, water, clothing, and shelter, I don't mean truffles, Perrier, Prada, and a McMansion. You can also live well with Ruffles, Pepsi, Payless, and a motorhome.

Some of you may argue, "I've worked hard. I deserve more than just the necessities for survival, because as Luke 10:7 says, 'The laborer deserves his wages.'"

As my grandfather used to say, "True 'nuf." But that mentality can also become a vicious cycle. We reward ourselves with things beyond what we actually need to the point that we can no longer tell the difference between necessities and luxuries. Soon we lose track of what is enough, which causes us to overwork, overload, and overstress. And then we find ourselves in direct conflict with another Bible verse, one of the Ten Commandments: "Remember the Sabbath Day, and keep it holy" (Exodus 20:8). We can't truly rest if we are constantly worried that we don't have enough. We can't truly share love if we are steeped in a perception of scarcity.

One way to break that cycle is to acknowledge what we have. Periodically, I like to pause and go through a list of five categories to remind myself of my blessings: health, means, love, beauty, and calling.

Health includes physical health and safety. Asking questions such as, "Did I wake up this morning?" can help us focus on our most basic blessings with laser precision.

Means is the ability to provide for yourself. Can I afford to buy groceries (including a ridiculous luxury like mac and cheese hotdogs)? Can I pay my rent? Acknowledging the blessing of having the means to pay for what you need transforms the mundane task of writing checks into a sacred ritual.

Love is the blessing of family, friendship, and community. Do I have people around me who love me, honor me, and treat me with respect? Acknowledging love is also about reminding ourselves of the unconditional spiritual love that we all receive. As God says to us in Isaiah 43:1, "I have called you by name; you are mine."

Beauty is anything that feeds the soul. Maybe you have a garden, or perhaps you have a Harley Davidson that you love. I have both in Wisconsin, but neither in New York City, so I give thanks for the wee plants in my apartment window and the tiny plastic model of a Harley Davidson Sportster on my desk.

Your calling is the reason you get up in the morning—a connection to something bigger than yourself. It could be your job or caring for your family or a loved one. Even if you are retired from your job and living alone, you still have a purpose. Your calling may be greeting the lonely person at the grocery store who is ignored by everyone else. Or it may be showing kindness to a telemarketer (unlike the rest of America). You matter, and for that, you should give thanks.

Will I give up my mac and cheese hotdogs? Maybe. Maybe not. What I will do is celebrate what they represent: the health that enables me to stand at the Weber and grill them, the means to buy them, the love of the family members who eat them, the beauty of the tiny pieces of pasta and cheese that ooze out, and the simple purpose of feeding body and soul. Most of all, I will try, before I even take a bite, to raise up a prayer of thanks and acknowledge that it is enough.

Questions to Consider:

- What things do you own that you don't need?
- Do you have enough? Why or why not?
- Do you have health, means, love, beauty, and calling? What can you do to share those blessings with others?

The King Lives!

"No, honey. I'm not the King. Christ is the King.
I'm just a singer."

- Elvis

Five years ago, my husband Toby and I made a pilgrimage to the Holy Land.

Memphis, Tennessee.

Yup, I said Memphis. Why? Because Memphis is the home of "The King," Elvis Presley. And for many, the King has reached an almost holy status.

I know this to be true from our tour of Graceland. As we waited in line for tickets under a sign that said "Enter the Blingdom," I turned to one of the guides and asked, "So, how long did Elvis live here before he died?"

The surrounding crowd gasped. The guide looked at me with shock and whispered, "We don't use the past tense here." She then pointed to her T-shirt, which read "Graceland, where Elvis LIVES."

It didn't matter that no one there had actually seen Elvis since he stopped walking the earth over forty years ago. Elvis fans don't care.

Without any concrete proof, they believe he lives. Elvis lives, baby. The King lives!

It's a shame we don't all have that kind of faith in our *heavenly* King. For with that faith (along with a few cupcakes and a shiny tiara), oh, how our lives might change.

For example, because Elvis fans believe he lives, they share their love of the King in all they do. They wear Elvis clothing, decorate their homes with Elvis paraphernalia, even water their yards with Elvis. In fact, my favorite item in the gift shop was an Elvis sprinkler that swivels his hips as he waters your grass.

What if we shared our faith that clearly? As 1 John 2:6 says, "Those who claim to belong to him must live just as Jesus did." If we believe the King lives, then we should share his love in every aspect of our lives.

Elvis fans also work to build community with other believers. There are over four hundred Elvis fan clubs worldwide. There are also Elvis churches, such as The First Presleyterian Church of Elvis the Divine. (That's not a typo. Google it if you don't believe me.)

Elvis fans understand the power of community, and so should we. Remember Jesus's words in Matthew 18:20: "Where two or three are gathered in my name, I am there among them." Living a life of faith is not easy. We need the support of others to stay strong and grounded on our journey.

Elvis fans serve as role models in another way, too: If you believe the King lives, you will actively seek him. Elvis fans are constantly looking for the King. And sometimes they find him! There have been Elvis sightings all over the world—from a spa in Tokyo to a Burger King in Michigan. There was even a woman who claimed that she saw Elvis's face in a taco shell at Chi-Chi's.

If we believe the King lives, we will seek him as Jesus commanded in Matthew 7:7: "Ask and it will be given to you; seek and you will find; knock and the door will be opened to you." If we begin to seek Christ truly, we, too, may start to see his face materialize in places we never saw him before, such as in the eyes of a stranger, the face of an immigrant, or the expression of someone who is hungry, thirsty, or homeless.

The Christian faith is not passive. It is a faith of action. It should make us want to bring in the kingdom—or the blingdom—or whatever it takes to ease the suffering of this world. Perhaps Elvis said it best: "Music and religion are similar because both should make you wanna move."

Sometime this week, find a quiet moment and ask yourself, "Do I believe?" From the deepest parts of your heart, the answer will surely come.

He lives. He lives, baby. The King lives!

Questions to Consider:

- Do you believe the King lives?

- Do you seek him?

- Do you share that faith and love in all you do?

Do It Now

"Dream as if you'll live forever.
Live as if you'll die today."

- James Dean

What's on your bucket list?

Don't have one?

Well, we need to change that right now.

Life is like a trip to the grocery store: If you don't have a list before you go, you end up leaving without the stuff you want and with a lot of stuff that you don't want.

We all have hopes and dreams. Maybe it's a trip you want to take, a book you want to write, a song you want to sing, a skill you want to learn, or a relationship you want to heal. Dreams are important! As the old saying goes, "Don't be pushed by your worries; be pulled by your dreams."

The problem is that we're always thinking, *I'll get to it later; I've got time.*

Newsflash: You don't.

Never take time for granted. Do it now!

Proverbs 27:1 says, "Do not boast about tomorrow, for you do not know what a day may bring." And if you need further proof, look at our daily headlines. Life can change in the blink of an eye.

The sad thing is that we waste so much of life's fleeting moments by doing pointless things like complaining. We complain about our parents and then miss the precious years we have left with them. We complain about our kids, and in the blink of an eye, they're grown and gone. We complain about getting old and taint the years we still have to enjoy life.

We can complain our way through an entire life. And then it's gone—never to return.

The flip side of the "I've got time" excuse is "It's too late." That justification comes clothed in many versions: "I'm too old." "The opportunity has passed." "People would think I'm crazy."

We've all done it.

But here's the truth of the matter: You can chase your dreams at any age, at any time. For example, F.X. Toole made his literary debut at seventy years old, his first novel being the basis for the movie *Million Dollar Baby*.

No one's saying that the path to your dream will be a straight line. Look at my road: trial lawyer to standup comedian and Baptist minister. In fact, one of the things I've learned as a comedian is that the ending of your act is the most important part. It doesn't matter if you bomb in the beginning of the set. Give people your best material at the end, and that's what they will remember.

The same is true in life. Even if you mess up in the beginning, make choices you regret, or let opportunities pass you by, if you give the world your best stuff at the end, that's what they'll remember.

Many of us have resigned ourselves to a life devoid of dreams. We walk this earth physically alive but dead of spirit, operating at the level of our social security number—existing rather than living. Hear me when I say this: Life is too precious to live it without dreams. It's never too late to change!

Whatever is important to you, whatever you feel passionate about doing in this life, don't take time for granted. Don't waste the gift you've been given.

Figure out what's at the top of your list. Remember your dream, and do it now!

Questions to Consider:

- Do you have a bucket list? If not, why not? If so, what's on it?

- Do you spend time complaining? About what?

- What dreams have you let die? Why?

- Make a list of three ways you can pursue those dreams NOW!

World Peace through Pulled Pork

"Barbeque may not be the road to world peace.
But it's a start."

- Anthony Bourdain

I'd like to spend the next two chapters talking about one of the most powerful ways to love: resolving conflict. To do so, I will use lessons from reconciliation sources that you would naturally expect: Barbecue and Las Vegas.

We start, as one must, with Barbecue.

I hail from a state that offers a no-fail plan for world peace. It's not from politicians or pundits, peaceniks or pedagogues. No, my friends, the secret lies in how the people of North Carolina have learned to live with a difference of opinion so deeply ingrained that it's almost genetically encoded. The bone of contention? Barbecue sauce.

If you didn't have the privilege of being raised in a BBQ-centric state, this may seem a bit far-fetched. But those of us who have lived with the tension, endured the heated debates, and been dismissed or demeaned because of our sauce preference know better.

To paraphrase Norman Maclean, the author of *A River Runs Through It*, there is no clear line between religion and [North Carolina barbecue]. And religion is something you don't monkey with.

Ever.

The sauce saga began over three hundred years ago with the introduction of a tangy, vinegar-based sauce—a vestige of Caribbean and West Indian influences that included vinegar, salt, and black and red pepper. The turning point came in 1876 when Heinz introduced a new-fangled concoction called ketchup. Soon after, the western part of the state, led by German immigrants in Lexington, North Carolina, began experimenting with a different, sweeter tomato-based sauce. Like a Baptist church that stopped lovin' Jesus, this was the ultimate blasphemy.

Brother began to turn against brother, family against family. Everyone jumped into the fray, and the name-calling continues to this day. For example, Dennis Rogers, a columnist, western sauce advocate, and the self-appointed "Oracle of the Holy Grub," once publicly referred to the eastern recipe as "imitation BBQ." At the other end of the spectrum, author Jerry Bledsoe, a rabid eastern sauce advocate and the self-professed "world's leading, foremost barbecue authority," once wrote in the *Raleigh News and Observer*, "People who would put ketchup in the sauce they feed to innocent children are capable of most anything."

This is war, and it's a war not unlike many of our modern headlines. In fact, most of our global problems break down into the same formula as the NC barbecue ruckus: someone is trying to mess with something that is "holy" to someone else.

Some people treat money like it's holy. Others give holy status to land, power, oil, truth, or barbeque sauce. Given this parallel, perhaps our global leaders might consider studying how North Carolinians have engaged in a generations-old fight without annihilating each other.

Our solution is quite simple. Step one: we remember what we have in common. North Carolinians may fight over the sauce, but in the end, we are all lovers of what it enhances: pulled pork. What if Democrats and Republicans tried this approach? Our two parties fight over, well, everything. But in the end—Democrats or Republicans—we're are all Americans.

Step two: North Carolinians realize that while we disagree on the means, the end goal is the same: we are all just trying to make a better barbecue sauce. What if we gave the same consideration to those who walk a different path? What if we *assumed* the good intentions of those who are different and offered them the benefit of the doubt?

Step three: We put all the sauces on the table and share a meal together. Oscar Wilde once said, "After a good dinner one can forgive anybody, even one's own relatives." I found out the truth of this statement growing up in Charlotte, the war-torn border of the barbecue wars, where we knew a thing or two about compromise. For example, during holiday dinners family members gathered around our table would include people from eastern *and* western North Carolina, South Carolinians (who worship a completely different, mustard-based sauce), and even, gasp, Texans, who prefer brisket to pulled pork. My mother, always the diplomat, would place all the different meats and sauces on the table, give one of her "looks" to the gathered barbecue enemies, then announce like a general on a battlefield, "Now sit down and eat. And let's agree to disagree."

And that, my friends, is how you accomplish world peace. Like mixing a beloved barbecue sauce, it takes a dash of diplomacy, a pinch of patience, and equal portions of empathy and respect. So, the next time you feel your blood pressure spiking over the daily news, imagine pulling up a chair, putting *all* the sauces on the table, and enjoying a meal with those with whom you disagree.

Questions to Consider:

- With whom do you have a conflict? With whom do you disagree?

- What is the common ground you might share?

- What if we assumed their good intentions and put aside our doubts?

Baptists in Vegas

"Las Vegas is the most honest fake city in the world."

- Frank Scoblete, *author*

I played Vegas.

As a Baptist minister.

Okay, so I offered a workshop for seven people ninety miles outside of Vegas.

Either way, that trip created one of the craziest combinations imaginable: a Baptist minister in Vegas! Think about that. It's like putting an Episcopalian in an improv troupe.

Vegas is nothing if not a series of crazy pairings. The town is one of humanity's tackiest and most garish creations, and it's situated in the midst of one of God's most beautiful creations—the Mojave Desert. There are gondolas in fake Venetian canals floating by Elvis impersonators. The Eiffel Tower stands proudly next to the Statue of Liberty. The Sphinx and the Great Pyramid tower over an IHOP. And my personal favorite: a billboard for the Mormon church appears next to one advertising an all-male dance revue from Australia called "Thunder from Down Under."

But from all these crazy things that seemingly have nothing in common, a city emerges—a community that bridges the differences and unifies them into one joyful, celebratory spirit. Tell me that isn't a lesson we need.

The joining together of unexpected things breaks open our way of seeing the world. It helps us approach situations in a fresh way. In fact, here's a statement I bet you never thought you'd hear: Vegas and Jesus have a lot in common.

Jesus knew how to jar people out of their comfortable places and challenge old images with what might have seemed like crazy pairings: the kingdom of God and a mustard seed; the weakest as the greatest; a banquet table where the honored guests were tax collectors, prostitutes, and sinners. His images still jar us today. They make us stop, reconsider, and reevaluate. It's like the old saying goes, "A comfort zone is a beautiful place, but nothing ever grows there."

When we jar our thinking, we shift our perspective. We begin to see and appreciate the marvelous diversity of God's creation, things like heaven and earth, platypus and blowfish, Jerry Springer and Jerry Falwell.

It's a crazy, wondrous variety, and yet a variety from the same creator. As the Apostle Paul said, "Now there are varieties of gifts, but the same Spirit; and there are varieties of services, but the same Lord; and there are varieties of activities, but it is the same God" (1 Corinthians 12:4-6).

Today, we are faced with factions, dividing lines, and anger. The only lens through which we seem to see is the lens of difference. And therein lies the problem—our current inability to see past the differences to our commonalities. I say current because we are capable of a much broader vision.

In addition to the Thunder from Down Under and Mormon Church billboards, I saw one featuring a photo of Abraham Lincoln with one of his most famous statements: "A house divided against itself cannot stand." Underneath that familiar quote was a new phrase: "Civility is in you. Pass it on." This was such a simple reminder, but one that hit me like a jet breaking the sound barrier. We have civility in us. Find it, remember it, and pass it on.

One of my favorite poets, Mary Oliver, asked in her poem, "The Summer Day":

Tell me,
what is it you plan to do
with your one
wild and precious life?

I can't imagine a better way to spend that wild and precious life than to love, and to dedicate yourself to seeing our commonalities first.

Baptists in Vegas? Why not.

If Elvis and the pyramids can come together to create an oasis in the desert, then what greater thing might we build if we bridge our differences and come together with one loving, celebratory spirit?

Questions to Consider:

- What is it you plan to do with your one wild and precious life?

- What bridges can you repair and/or build in your family? What common ground can you find between factions in your community? What connections can you make in this broken world?

- Is civility in you? If so, how do you pass it on?

Wisdom from the Kmart

"The only person you are destined to become is the
person you decide to be."

- Ralph Waldo Emerson

When I want to lift myself out of the dumps, I go to the Astor Place
Kmart in the East Village of New York City. Sure, I could default to
other solutions, like walking around Central Park, watching a rerun
of *Chopped*, or, on a particularly bad day, breaking out the French
onion soup packet, sour cream, and Ruffles.

But my first choice is the Kmart.

Specifically, I favor an area in the far back corner of the Kmart
basement. It is devoid of windows or natural light and has a back
wall of clear glass that faces the dark, dungeon-like tunnel of the
Number 6 Subway train. There, you will find the most unexpected
of things—a plant nursery.

Sprouting in this dreary prison are woven ficus trees, begonias,
African violets, scheffleras, Christmas cacti, and spindly spider
plants. I feel so sorry for those little plants. They struggle to grow in
their stale, lifeless chamber. And if the fake light isn't bad enough,
every five minutes the train roars by, shaking them to the base of
their wee roots.

That's why every once in a while, I head to the Kmart to stage a prison break for a few lucky leafy inmates, so that they might recover in my home (or, given my gardening abilities, die in peace).

But at least they have a chance. And that's all we as humans want, too.

Our environment is not so different from that of the plants in the basement of the Kmart. We live surrounded by toxicity, in places where we are often denied light, love, and sustenance, places where we can be shaken to our roots by unforeseen circumstances.

Although we sometimes give up in the face of such obstacles, those wee plants continue to fight, to use whatever they have to stay alive, and to stretch their roots and strain their stems to convert even the tiniest bit of artificial light into energy and life.

One of the reasons I love rescuing them is the tiny plastic tab that peeks out of each plant's pot. On it is an image of what that plant could grow into if it receives proper light and care, an image of its true potential.

We all have that same divine potential—that metaphorical plastic tab with our best self embossed on it. And sometimes we need a reminder of what that looks like so we don't lose our way, which is all too easy to do in this world.

Our true potential has nothing to do with what anyone else's "plant tab" looks like. Consider the marigolds in the Kmart. They don't try to grow into another kind of flower, like a rose. They don't question whether they deserve love or whether they are valued or paid enough. Their only quest is to grow into that one unique image appearing on their little plastic tab, to evolve into their divine potential.

The next time you are feeling low, consider a little wisdom from the basement of the Astor Place Kmart. Find a place in your community where you can rescue an imprisoned plant. Or better yet, rescue another person who finds him or herself trapped in a toxic place with little light or love. Maybe you reach out to a friend in need. Or perhaps you volunteer at a homeless shelter or nursing home. Or maybe you write a letter to our troops, veterans, and first responders through organizations such as Operation Gratitude. Reaching out to others can do wonders to help them—and you— grow.

The Benedictine nun Joan Chittister once said that we have the potential to be the human beat of the heart of God. Don't waste that gift. Don't give up the fight because you find yourself in an unhealthy, unsupportive place. Each one of us has a divine potential. We just need to stretch our mind, body, and soul towards its light and do what we were born to do: love.

Questions to Consider:

- If you had a plastic plant tab for how you would look with a nourishing environment, what would it look like?

- What are the things that block our light and air?

- What is your divine potential? What gift does the world need that God has bestowed upon you?

STAY IN TOUCH!

I hope you have enjoyed my book and found some new joy, pride, and love in your life. Now we've got to keep it going! Here are some ways:

SIGN UP for my FREE biweekly newsletter, the *Shiny Side Up*, which shares infectious inspiration that will lift you up, make you smile, and leave you stronger! http://susansparks.com/connect/

READ more of my books.

Try my award-winning first book *Laugh Your Way to Grace: Reclaiming the Spiritual Power of Humor*. Featured by *O, The Oprah Magazine*, this book shares a humorous, yet substantive look at the power of humor in transforming our life, work, and spiritual path.

My second book, *Preaching Punchlines: The Ten Commandments of Comedy*, shares how the tools of standup comedy can transform preaching—and all forms of communication.

Or how about generating some Christmas cheer any time of the year? Then try my best-selling and multiple award–winning book, *Miracle on 31st Street: Christmas Cheer Any Time of the Year— Grinch to Gratitude in 26 Days!*

Why not jump-start your gratitude? Then, try my joy journal with inspirational scriptures *Grace-Filled Gratitude: A 40-Day Joy Journal with Inspirational Scriptures.*

WATCH and LISTEN to my weekly sermon broadcast every Sunday at 11a.m. EST from the historic Madison Avenue Baptist Church in New York City.
http://mabcnyc.org/worship/live-streaming/ Or subscribe to our sermon podcast and listen later at your convenience.

GATHER. Form a reading group in your community and use the book as a guide. Make sure to serve cupcakes and wear tiaras when discussing it!

INVITE me to guest preach or speak (live or virtually) in your community! I'd love to share some joy!

LIKE/FOLLOW my Facebook and Instagram pages (links on SusanSparks.com) where you'll find more joy and gratitude ideas. And maybe consider sharing about the book on social media! There is a sample chapter on my website you can share with your friends.

SHARE. If this book has brought joy to your life, share it with others. Show them some love! Send them a note, tell them how much they mean to you, and include the book as a gift (or at least let them borrow it ☺).

POST A REVIEW. If you enjoyed the book (or even if you didn't) I would so appreciate a review on Amazon! Honest reviews are super important for the success of the book. So take a moment and please add your opinion! MANY thanks!

For more ways to keep in touch, check out my website: SusanSparks.com.

I look forward to hearing from you!

Now . . . claim your joy, shine your radiance,
and go do what you were meant to do!

AUTHOR BIO

As a trial lawyer turned standup comedian and Baptist minister, Susan Sparks is America's only female comedian with a pulpit. A North Carolina native, Susan received her B.A. at the University of North Carolina, law degree from Wake Forest University, and her Master of Divinity at Union Theological Seminary in New York City.

Currently the senior pastor of the historic Madison Avenue Baptist Church in New York City (and the first woman pastor in its 170-year history), Susan's work with humor, healing, and spirituality have been featured in *O, The Oprah Magazine;* the *New York Times;* and on such networks as ABC, CNN, CBS, and the History Channel.

A featured TEDx speaker and a professional comedian, Susan tours nationally with a stand-up Rabbi and a Muslim comic in the Laugh in Peace Tour. In addition to her speaking and preaching, Susan is the best-selling author of five books, and an award-winning nationally syndicated columnist through the USA Today Network.

Most importantly, Susan and her husband, Toby, love to fly-fish, ride their Harleys, eat good barbecue, and root for North Carolina Tarheel basketball and the Green Bay Packers.

Find out more about Susan at SusanSparks.com!

FAVORITE CUPCAKE RECIPES!

Dr. Pepper Cupcakes
https://www.countryliving.com/food-drinks/recipes/a43417/dr-pepper-cupcakes-recipe/

Heavenly Creme-filled Cupcakes
https://www.foodnetwork.com/recipes/ree-drummond/heavenly-creme-filled-cupcakes-recipe-2178896

Mini Heath Bar Cheesecakes (sorta cupcakes . . . but I LOVE THEM!)
https://www.bitememore.com/easy-recipes/mini-heath-bar-cheesecakes-recipe

Chocolate Key Lime Cupcakes
https://www.southernliving.com/syndication/chocolate-key-lime-cupcake-pies

Knock-You-Naked Margarita Cupcakes
https://fatmamastamales.com/knock-you-naked-margarita-cupcakes-recipe/

Turner's Blackberry Buttercream Cupcakes
Blackberries on blackberries, this dessert is chocked full and guaranteed to take any blackberry lover to heaven. I modified this version which originally called for raspberries for the filling and used plain, vanilla buttercream. You can also skip the filling part, if you just want to go for a lighter, frosted version of these cupcakes.

VANILLA CUPCAKES
1 box vanilla cake mix
3 large eggs
½ cup butter, melted
1 cup water

BLACKBERRY FILLING
2 full cups frozen unsweetened blackberries,
thawed with ¼ cup sugar
1/3 cup sugar
1 ¼ cups water
3 tablespoons corn starch
1 teaspoon lemon juice

BLACKBERRY BUTTERCREAM
½ cup butter, softened
½ cup fresh blackberries
1 teaspoon vanilla extract
1 teaspoon lemon zest
1/8 teaspoon salt
1 (16 oz.) package plus 1 cup powdered sugar

To make cupcakes: Preheat oven to 350°F and place 24 cupcake papers in a muffin pan.

Melt the butter in the microwave. Add cake mix, eggs and water to the butter in large bowl and mix on low for 1 min. Then, mix on high for 1 min.

Fill cupcake papers. Place cupcakes on middle rack in the oven for 20 minutes (or until inserted toothpick comes out clean). Let cool.

To make filling: If there is any juice in your blackberries, drain the juice into a measuring cup and then fill cup with water until you have 1¼ cup of liquid in total. In a medium saucepan, combine water, sugar, flour and lemon juice and mix well. Heat and stir until mixture boils and thickens. Cool completely. Stir in thawed blackberries.

Cut out a small cone shaped section in the center of the cooled cupcakes add filling to the hole, then replace the tops.

To make buttercream frosting: Wash and thoroughly dry fresh blackberries. Beat first all ingredients except powdered sugar at medium speed with an electric mixer until creamy.

Gradually add powdered sugar, beating at low speed until blended and smooth after each addition.

Add frosting to a pastry bag with your favorite tip and frost cupcakes.

Made in the USA
Columbia, SC
27 May 2021